HOMESI

C000292087

Homesickness And Exile

EDITED BY RACHEL PIERCEY AND EMMA WRIGHT

with poems from Ivy Alvarez, Zeina Hashem Beck,
Alex Bell, Carole Bromley, Mary Buchinger, George
David Clark, James Coghill, Ellie Danak, Cath Drake,
Frank Dullaghan, John Froy, Charlotte Higgins, Holly
Hopkins, Elizabeth Horne, Anja Konig, Eve Lacey,
Gill Learner, Rachel Long, Marissa Mazek, John
McCullough, Cheryl Moskowitz, Selina Nwulu,
Richard O'Brien, Lisa Ortiz, Rachel Piercey, Stephen
Sexton, Vili Skarlopoulou and James Trevelyan

THE EMMA PRESS

THE EMMA PRESS

First published in Great Britain in 2014
by The Emma Press Ltd

ISBN 978-1-910139-02-8

A CIP catalogue record of this book
is available from the British Library.

Printed and bound in Great Britain
by Jasprint, Washington.

theemmapress.com
editor@theemmapress.com

CONTENTS

LIST OF ILLUSTRATIONS

PREFACE

Part of the appeal in reading the Classics is seeing what still resonates today. Feeling something in response to words written in a completely different culture over two thousand years ago creates a connection across the millennia and raises fascinating, sometimes disturbing, questions about what it means to be human.

When the Roman poet Ovid was ejected from Rome by the emperor Augustus and sent to Tomis, a remote town on the Black Sea, he wrote five books of poetry in an attempt to bring about his pardon. These books, the *Tristia*, describe his last night in Rome, his terrifying journey across stormy seas, his misery in Tomis, his abandoned wife and friends, his early life and poetic works, and – above all – his hope that Augustus will relent and let him come back to Rome.

Ovid's heartbroken descriptions of his wife and friends will resonate with anyone who has ever had to leave behind a loved one, but for me the fascination lies in Ovid's unwavering belief in where his home is. He's been banished from it by Augustus and he'll live the rest of his days in Tomis, but his home will always be in Rome – not where he was born, but where he chose to live, surrounded by his wife, friends, library, reputation and personal history. In a very callous way, I feel envious of Ovid in his absolute conviction in where he calls home, because it strikes me as quite rare and wonderful to be able to identify somewhere as your home with full satisfaction and accuracy. Ovid may have lost it, but he had it to begin with: somewhere he was happy to belong.

When we launched the call for poems for this book, I wondered what we would learn about modern attitudes to home and whether Ovid's feeling of bereavement would be echoed in any of the poems. In the privileged world of cheap flights and Skype, people can, in theory, go wherever they like, come back and visit often, and stay in touch via the Internet. Do people even feel homesick like Ovid anymore?

In the poems we collected, the concept of 'home' appears to be problematic, at once more flexible and more elusive than it is for Ovid. In Holly Hopkins's 'England, where did you go?' and Alex Bell's 'The Town', the speakers seem ill at ease with the place all indicators would suggest is their home, while in Selina Nwulu's 'Homecoming' and Frank Dullaghan's 'Dundalk' the speakers feel divided between the common signifiers of what a home should be: where you are born, where your parents are from, where you grew up and where you live now.

Even when the speaker is clearly away from home, I get the sense that a return to their nominal home would not dispel the restlessness. In James Coghill's 'One Morning, Borås' and George David Clark's 'Prodigalia', homesickness and foreignness seem to be a state of mind, to do with feeling something is missing wherever you are. Similarly, the traveller in Elizabeth Horne's 'Coming down' is torn between the excitement of new lands and the allure of home.

The poems which chime the most with Ovid's are the ones where the speakers acknowledge the existence of something which makes them feel accepted, safe and content. In John McCullough's 'The Restaurant at One Thousand Feet', this is a person, the emigrant Canadian addressee, while in Richard O'Brien's 'Forgetting How to Swim' home is dry land, somewhere the speaker doesn't just survive but can flourish.

Home, as Ovid implies throughout the *Tristia*, is wherever you choose to call your home, not just where you were born or where you happen to be. In *Homesickness and Exile*, we see the difficulties this raises, as people struggle to choose and fail to escape homes which have been imposed on them. Ovid's miserable, completely reluctant journey to Tomis (which I've depicted in my illustrations) contrasts with the more ambiguous attitudes of travellers in *Homesickness and Exile*, but ultimately the poets are united across the millennia by their profound desire to be somewhere they know they belong.

Emma Wright
WINNERSH
August, 2014

HOMESICKNESS AND EXILE

LIGHT ON THE GALACTIC TIDE

for Jyothish

You streak through, irregular comet,
surf in from the outer rim of Chamaeleon.
You barely hold on to the centre, tenuous gravity;
you are Lemmon, an astronomical whim.

You are comical, out of context
in any galaxy. You are brave; planets play it safe.
You dare to be a cosmic phenomenon,
diamond in the coal mine of the universe.

You visit, ephemeral guest, travelled light years
to get here. But you can't stay.
Your visa says *temporary at best*.
Foreigner is the fate that fits.

Dirty snowball of wit, you imprint
your one-of-a-kind mind, instrument for detecting
the angle on everything. You chisel
your singular trajectory into the sky.

You are the one cone in an elliptic world,
an acorn in the company of melons.
You ride your eccentric orbit close to the sun.
You know you can never go home.

Dundalk

This is the town that I left, its high-
ceilinged classrooms, the smell and weight
of a new year's school books,
the De La Salle brothers with their canes
beating learning into working class boys,
the wrought-iron gate to the train station,
a portal to elsewhere, the churches dark
with silences, that one hip northern priest with
his good looks, who came to the house
when my pregnant sister got married,
for the small after-meal my mother put out,
who refused to acknowledge the figure of shame
that padded about and sat between us
but belted out his voice in song to celebrate
the union, the coming child, and filled us
with the extraordinary knowledge
of ordinary things. This is the town where
my brother came home once broken
and bloody, where I first cupped the marvel
of a girl's breast, earned money, drank.
This is the town where I dreamed
of the possible in its many coats, though
never once dreamed myself dressed and away
from the accents and small certainties
of that parish. It is the town where my mother
finally let go of herself, where my brother's
heart gave out, where my father died slowly,
becoming more insubstantial with each sin
he acknowledged in himself. This is the town
that I left, a town where my sisters still live,
anchoring it to its past, as it grows a bright
new plumage and tries to fly away from me.

Homecoming

We're going home she said
and I think *At last*
I'm tired of this town
Its stares never got used to me
and this place feels like a cold scowl

I leave the monochrome
for a tsunami of Nigerian colour
I am hit by its everything:
airport lines of waiting
duelling haggles
dense smells swathed in dust
exhaling rhythms

The heat wraps its legs around me
pees in the small of my back
I stick to the seat of the car
before it throws me up and down
a yo-yo over potholes

The village (my village?) is waiting for me
its arms stretched like palm trees
for the wanderer returning
They are waving for my homecoming

The language (my language?) speaks in songs
woven with echoes and blood ties
I am out of tune
The meanings ducking out of my hands

I am the mosquitoes' new fruit
a different taste in a familiar shape
They suck from me the authenticity
my words cannot give
I am raw bitten and grateful

Can I have this?
Can I make this place my own?
I say hello in Igbo to a face I should recognise
She cackles at my attempts

I have fallen between the gaps
I mourn this abyss between two hands
and smell the red clay soil in the cracks of my palms
Welcome home, darling

Yellow Sea Night

Note how   if the conditions are right
the swell of the night lulls the dog
to sleep   usually wheezing
and peaking with a sickness
she can't understand   see her curled
in the passage where tanned crew   skin
cracked by Gobi sand blown east
in great clouds   offer pats on their way
to bed   and above   on deck
told to keep an eye on any change   is Kai
two hundred miles from home and three weeks
on lates   tonight he thinks
only of his wife left behind who   for fish
and sand and food   has been cleft
from his side   feels in his hand the torch
her ankle joint   the gentle
throb of the hull   her hips
the curve of the wale   her arching back
water lapping at its edges   lips

EMIGRANT

He left by easy stages, as if
that way we wouldn't notice.
The first time only for six weeks,
missed June days in the garden,
his dog growing older, grandpa's funeral.

The second time just for a year
and he'd be back before we knew it,
wrote long letters on airmail paper,
missed Alan Partridge, rugby league,
a pint of John Smith's.

The third time it was final; parcelled up
every trace of himself, filled six boxes
to go by freight next day: his saxophone,
Return of the Jedi, Charley Parker,
Deacon Blue, Guns'n'Roses, Madonna.

In the end the CDs never made it,
filched by some deckhand, customs officer
or delivery man who now strolls,
whistling those tunes down avenues
of eucalyptus, screeched at by cockatoos.

FOREIGN

A cement-block house down a grassy lane,
this shy woman, Rosa, who will hand-scrub and iron our underwear,
her fierce child, the youngest, naked, except for a torn t-shirt
slung caveman-style across one thin shoulder, but mostly this bed
 – our bed – in the middle of their main room, humming
beneath a canopy of flies – the only language we all can follow –
and these next few months in this, our second year of marriage.

Children appear from nowhere, crowd around us, eagerly await
the unclicking of the suitcases. We say *hola*, one of a dozen words
we know in Spanish, and our audience titters. The bed is smaller
than the scored dining table it has replaced, narrower than
the two of us side by side. We'll spoon in desperation, our feet
sticking out the end like Li'l Abner's, but in three dimensions,
tangled flesh on a bony bed, corporal fight over real estate.

Kids, cats, pigs wander in, dogs chase across our shared pillow.
Somehow, this isn't foreign. No, we are. We become someone else
as we take turns changing clothes beneath the sheets, sheets stained
with fleabite blood, our eyes vigilant watching doorless doorways.
We must say something, I plead, as if we had the words. *If not a door,
at least a curtain, it must be in the dictionary.* Sleep's private kingdom!
Ya mismo, Soon, is what we are learning in this country of *Manana* –

Tomorrow – a sky of promise where everything may change. *Manana*
splashes freely, laps up the warped legs of our little bed, threatens the fleas
drunk on my blood, pledges a clean blanket, a room with walls, maybe even
a bed that fits us. Sick of *manana*, I turn on you, oh husband, you foreign sore.
I knock on your heart, suspecting fleas, a font of fleas, whose bite I attract.
I dream in a language neither of us understands of a marriage
turned spider – menacing, strange – legs so fragile, frantic with webs.

ITHACA, NY

My first day
I found a place to live,
a rooming house.
The fridge was one flight up
where no one lived
but boys,
nocturnal predators
who ate my cheese
and left behind
just teeth marks,
socks and cigarette ash.
That summer
I got my Nissan,
discovered it was forbidden
to swim in public lakes
because the town
was worried you would sue them
when you drowned.

Prodigalia

When I first furnished my suite in the city
I had a cashmere hammock
slung between the tusks of a tremendous elephant
whose bust was mounted on the bedroom wall.
In that prodigious net young ladies
from the delta used to tumble like rabbits.
I could feel their hearts, like rabbits' hearts,
beating through their chests,
and imagine, with some encouragement,
that I was God.

And there was too the elephant himself:
the leather blankets of his ears
that I'd detach to draw around my shoulders
while I slept; the hidden compartment
in his trunk where I kept a meerschaum pipe
and petty cash; the eye marbles – colour of the lowest
gas flames – through which he glowered at me
his great suspicion, and, now and then,
flashed forth a look of obliterating tenderness
not unlike a father's.

One Morning, Borås

I suddenly realised I had too much time to think,
in the wide, bright streets, not a single verb
of English to interrupt

save for the occasional 'damn' or 'fuck'
or line lifted from some American sitcom
I probably would not care for.

It is my day off, but I still drink more coffee
than I should, crave the mastic buzz
of twice boiled grounds

eaten with a spoon. Beating the lunchtime rush,
I duck into a café for fikar, eat
kanelbullar, quiver

into my fourth cup of the day, losing myself
to a menagerie of daydreams
that surface in the shape

of leafy seadragons, solenodons, aye-ayes
or *gocea ohridana*, rare
gastropod endemic

to a tiny patch of mud at the bottom of Lake Ohrid,
tucked up in their torn quilt sanctuary,
drowning in silt.

Distracted, I leave without paying, drift out
into the crowd in search
of sculptures:

Catafalque outside the högskola, Bodhi
in the Viskan, a gun with a knot
in it and a giant rabbit

that smirks cartoonishly as I settle down
to watch the stadspark, its London plane
and lime trees; the people

like scrawls of people, the commonplace
contingent of pigeons and jackdaws,
my copy of *I Studied Once…*

and a dog-eared phrasebook I've learnt
off by heart, just in case I meet someone
who wants to talk.

PARIS, TEXAS

I woke and the bed was on fire.
                 I walked
                         I walked the road
         until it wasn't road any more.

The land grew brown   spread flat
                        as batter
           spitting on its griddle.

I kept on my blazer.

       There was a twang
             like a pick to the ribcage
and it was blue
        but I wasn't sad.

                  There are memories
flammable as celluloid
           little as the water
               in my warm canteen.

        Skin burnt red
mind bleached clean.

                If you are somewhere
you are behind glass
       desert-blonde
           intensely fuzzed in hot pink mohair.

Coming down

For weeks and weeks we mouthed the word,
kept it on our tongues like a smooth pebble
or an ulcer, loving and loathing the texture,
tasting ahead the pleasure of re-belonging
and the boredom. Home.
The idea fizzed like sherbet in our mouths,
sweet and exciting, then gunged in our gums.
We couldn't leave it alone.
Great – home. Shit – home. Great shit.
Paris suddenly seemed cobwebby and conceited,
a sexy old sophisticate unable to comprehend
the allure of the unkempt libertine, unable to
compete with the divine ordinariness
of Australia. She sulked in stony grey silences
for five days straight, then flashed a defiant
thin blue thigh sky as we were leaving…

Mzungu

When you arrive, *Karibu*, to a fug of sweat
and a hot yellow sun and you set your feet
on a hard earth floor with the smell of dung
and dark red dust that clogs your nose. When
you do not know but pretend you do, the black
man's song and the women's dance, the thick
damp air, and mosquito hum. When you say
your name but it's not the same as the one they
chose before you came, *Mzungu*. When a child's
shaved head makes you touch your own wild
nest of hair and you feel unclean, your ways
obscene, *Habari njema* you want to say,
the news is good, *I'm well, all's well* –
your white words bob on the ocean swell.

Away

Back home my father's having a brain scan.
He's afraid they'll find something
and lock him up. I'm admiring a view
in Umbria, looking out over tiles
shaped like hotel curls of butter.

I've left that other me behind. They say
it could arrive any day. Domani perhaps,
or dopodomani. The airline has a new scam
to cut costs. It leaves your luggage at Stansted.
Surely it should be enough to deposit you
beside a pool with what you stand up in,
a passport, a few hundred euro,
a breeze in the olive grove, a lizard on a wall?

The sky is every different shade of blue,
white almost, where it meets the mountains
I can't photograph. I have no palette
to mix the greens of cedar, bay and almond,
no fine tip to trace a criss-cross orchard,
that avenue of cypress leading to a farm.

They'll be sliding my father out now
from a machine like a mortuary drawer.
They'll unhinge his visor, let him go,
then start to examine the tell-tale gaps
where memories were; the pier at Saltburn,
the cliff-lift, the way we pressed our noses
on the glass to watch the sea rise
to meet us, slate-grey edged with white.

Exile

You become a revolutionary
the day you turn your head from south to east
until the dizziness settles in your bones
and becomes a country
a passport
the hollow cornerstone of your heart
when anyone asks you of home.

You think to carve yourself a nationality
and so you build up a house from your bones
with your femurs for eaves
and your spine for the frame
and your skull on the door to keep strangers away.
You find
when it is made
that there is nothing left of you to live inside –
everything lost in construction.

Barbed wire borders your heart
and there are check points
at the sharp point of your rib cage
and men with guns
who ask the country of origin of your birth marks.
All dark skin and hard eyes
they scrutinize the road map of your veins –
don't they realize
that blood can never lead you home again.

Women of Corinth,

'there's no place like home' is my mantra, shrieked
with a throat that's sea-parched, spluttering dust;
I'm tapping these damn patent shoes till they wreak
red nomad havoc on that homewrecking lust
of my homemaker Jason, fleecing me
blind. Swear, Aegeus, pledge me a room
that childlessness may help me to flee:
give me four walls and I'll give you a womb.
What barren land that exiles mothers! Let
the record show it's them that double-glazed
your eyes and left my children all bereft
when all my wits turned vagabond, depraved
of them, my parting gift of pumpkin kids,
teeth like keys and eyes alight in broken heads.

Aunty

The cleaner eats her dinner against the tampon dispenser.
I can tell by the skin, the white meat of her bite, it's a Granny Smith.
She strips it to its spine, twists the stalk with her teeth,
tips brown beads into her palm, pockets them, bins the rest.
She catches me staring at her in the mirror,
'You thought I eat core like a savage?'
'No!' I pump soap, blast the dryer.
She kisses her teeth, laughs, *hmms* at the same time,
from the same mouth.
I thought only my Mum could do that.

Tannoy crackles, a god in the walls; there's a leak in the Men's.
She rises, sways, steadies herself on the sink.
I ask if she's ok. A pause.
A gap, generation wide, ocean sized –
I should address a woman this age as Aunty.
Are you ok, Aunty? But we're not related.
She raises her eyebrows, closes her eyes,
tries to kiss her nose with her lips.
This means yes, weary *yes*.
It's the face my Mum makes to the offer of tea
when she comes home from her night shift.
Lurid green and white badges smiling for them,
Here to assist YOU! branded across their buckets, their breasts.
'Me, I'm OK O. Jus' a little back pain.'
In her Yoruba accent I hear 'Jus' a little black pain.'

She stoops low for her bucket; I try to help her
but it's already scooped in deft hands,
hands I know if turned over
would have lifelines deep as knifewounds,
bistre as the vaccine scar on her fleshy arm.
She raises the bucket high, higher,

grey water sloshing, up on her head.
My eyes must widen, ready to bullfrog –
her laugh saves their amber rolling down my face, across the wet floor.
'Look at you, British girl.
You think we put any bucket on our head?'

I want to tell her *No, no, I know you don't,*
want to tell her a secret,
my Mum is Yoruba, or she was,
but 'Aunty' will ask *What people? What town?*
I won't be able to answer.
A red sun will creep up my neck, set on both sides of my face.
She'll be disappointed, know my ignorance,
my guilty sweep of a darker side under a carpet of Dad's white skin.

She resumes making a sea around my shoes,
leaves me an island. I stay silent,
listening to her wet mop slap tiles
like an awkward tongue.

Tannoy bellows louder this time.
'Moogee, we need you in the Men's NOW.'
I have a cousin called Moji,
I wonder if it meant to call the same name?
She told me it meant endless wealth,
whilst we sat at a bus stop sharing a box of chicken and chips.
Moji, she must be, grabs her mop and bucket,
muttering something to herself, or the god in the walls,
then stops at the door, shouts over her shoulder:
'When you see your Mom, my sistah, greet har for me.
A fine, fine daughter with a head full of nothing.
Tell har to tek you to Nigeria. They will fill it for you good.'
My laugh echoes foreign against the lockers.

Hiding from a Mouse

Ana was late, so I opened up.
The mouse was on the kitchen step,
legs, flank and the side of his face
glued to a paper trap.

He looked so soft, strained to rise
then fell into himself, trying to catch
tiny shivering breaths.

He didn't have the purchase
of stump-legged pigeons
who tear their feet off to escape,
didn't have their weight.

I shut the kitchen door,
took the chairs down from the tables,
put out the thin glass pots of salt and pepper.

Ana made no fuss when she arrived:
drowned it in a saucepan.
She came from the former Yugoslavia;
to her we all seemed like children.

On Rosebery Avenue

A London taxi firm *wants rivers.*
The Thames here doesn't cut it –

the water turns it back on such
modern flanks, and shuts

it light eyes – so the cabs
are navigating out, around the M25

and then further, falling
along the tarred burr

out of knowledge, to where
the tributaries of the road

are mysteries, but the air
smells of river, and the trees

grow with river, and they find it,
skating over soft banks,

their black pates slipping under,
their lights out to signify
this final shining passenger.

Coming Home

Krakow
where a gaunt dragon swallows coins
straight off a child's hand

where a beggar's finger points at my bag
and memories sail over rooftops past sleeping bells

where tired ghosts of pigeons past
land on cars, trodden stones and my arms

where, once upon a time, men and women marched
rewriting history with fists made of clay

where, as a girl, I wanted to set the world on fire
then grew up and joined the snaky queue
to the International Departure Lounge.

Today I am back, biting
into local bread, a cumin seed
stuck between my teeth.

The Town

The town holds a yearly festival of bloom.
It wears its blossoms like an elaborate hat
and fences cinch it in.

The town is quietly concerned about immigration.
It drums its fingers and reproaches greengrocers
for buying imported strawberries.

The town fills paper bags with Cox's Orange Pippins
and likes to know where the pork was raised.
The town refuses Scottish currency.

The town advertises itself as *Hardy Country*
and does not think of infanticide, sheep spilling off cliffs,
or a bloodspot thickening in the fibres of a ceiling.

The town owns a model of itself in the 1940s.
The tiny streets are the same, but there is no Sainsbury's.
The people are wooden pegs in woollen tank tops.

The town respects its elders and its dead.
Encourages ramps and bungalows, cream teas.
Each November, sticks itself with poppies.

The town likes doing crosswords under stories
on community gardens. It shudders at *London*.
It cannot fathom *abroad*.

The town wraps me tight as swaddling.
Later it does up my laces and ties my tie in a Windsor knot.
It despairs at my slovenliness and lack of effort.

The town dislikes my smart mouth
and tells me to smile, it might never happen.
Nothing happens.

When I came to the town I brought things with me
from outside, and the town took them
for my own good.

It keeps them in its locked top drawer.
It might return them
when I've learned to behave like an adult.

ARIEL

No one ever told you
that you cannot sing these new words
any more than a man can waltz on the surface of the sea

No one ever told you
that in this new language there is no poetry
that will fit in the shape of your lips

You see, this language
has another word for beauty –
things don't sound this way where you come from

So you stand in your fishnets and knife-edge heels
and you learn how to kiss with your new tongue
and they tell you *You taste of salt*
and they say *The women
in our country do not talk this way*

But no one ever said
that the language you'd known
that was easy as air
words tattooed on your bones
the language as dark as the country you're from
would be uprooted –
torn like a hook from your tongue

That new words would be sharper than you've ever known
would be bright as a pearl
bright as sea foam.

What Greta Garbo Offered

The ferry docks and I disembark
for water, something to umber
my gaze, disguise my fair hair. I brave the salty air.
                              The light is a slap.
Sand-grains clap-barnacle ankles, soles,
grit fingertips, these cheekbones.
Waves lap loud, teasing with my favourite word:
                              alone   *alone*   *alone*

Here, I am an island on an island off an island off Auckland.

Riding the curve of the world, I score
kinship with seagulls begging, sparrows inching
towards my outstretched hand. Listen. A raw delight
                              rises in them,
feathers dawning. In dark pocket corners, I'm forgetting
cake crumbs, two coins, an old perfume evanescing.

The Restaurant at One Thousand Feet

CN Tower, Toronto

on Lake Ontario small boats curve north and south
as the forest of your smile extends its boundaries

we have returned to the city of your birth
and spread our pockets' treasure on a table's landscape

a puddle of dollars keys like axes at rest
a bone of flint from Sussex with the Channel inside

I am in your atmosphere and may I say
you carry a lot of oxygen around you

a private sky as boundless as this country we float over
the dogged 401 cardinals, black squirrels

though we bring our own colours the grained slate of your eyes
pink fingertips that can turn a man to lemonade

while you tell me you remember only pancake maps
your childhood's rivers and islands of syrup

no one else is in the restaurant so late in the day
and getting dark very dark

but our plates are full as we stare down
at clouds migrating like herds of caribou

racing soundlessly into the distance glorious
as, secretly, they are all the time

Winged Carrots

You call them guardians,
these winged carrots
graffitied on the walls,
because you know
they take flight in your sleep,
land on rooftops, on clotheslines,
shield orphaned dreams
with their little black wings.

You call it the sign
because you have to look up
towards the sky to notice
it says 'Rooms for Rent'.
It is white, it rusts
from an old balcony;
the Arabic letters flake.

You call him Thyme
because he sweeps his bakery,
gathers the day, the *zaatar* dust,
always at the same hour.
'Bonjour,' he chants,
no matter what the time is,
as if words could lift
the falling darkness.

You call it orange,
this elevator with painted walls,
because in a city where walls
yield, where rails rust,
where litter fills the streets

like abandoned punctuation,
it has managed to keep
its colour.

You call it god, this sidewalk,
because you carry it with you everywhere:
in your pockets, your footsteps.
You've memorized its bends like a prayer,
its long silver-grey hair,
its cigarettes, its favourite
songs and curse words,
the holes in its shirts.

You call it evening
because of the way the rain
seeps through the streetlights,
carries some of their radiance, drips
on the green garbage bags,
on the bottles your neighbour lines outside.

You call it Beirut
because you have no other name
for the way trees and antennas tilt in the wind,
the wind always, the certainty of the wind.

The boy travels

home
                                        floats

            on the edges
of his memory
selecting for itself
moments
of uncommon warmth
already   passed
collaging   faces that have
lit
briefly
in the familiarity of
a landscape
that is after all
only   a   pattern
on the surface
of that particular
earth
the vague pleasure of
recognition
earned   so dearly
by remaining
long
enough

finding
a fresh sheet of paper
seeing from   here
that he was a stranger
there
too

drawing
what he knows
or hopes to know
in careful   detail
knowing too
that what he knows
interferes
meddles
with everything
he sees

wondering
how   to compose
best
the drifting
                  colours
yearning not
for a letter from home
but
for a box
of artist's quality
pencils

The Terminal Building

Already it's not Australia
though duty-free shops sell
coasters of aboriginal art,
didjeridus that would have to go
as hand luggage, giant frogs
that croak as we pass.

At the gate you hand me my laptop,
I touch your hair. We hug,
the little boy at playgroup
who never moved from the curtain
and the mother who didn't know
what to do in the empty house.

Leaving Perth, October 2012

The last day has a slow run-up: I take winding steps,
    notice the shimmer of sun on everything.
The last day stands in front of me staring at its moon watch,
    blinking its brightest morning.

The last day a cluster of people keep saying: *what –*
    are you leaving now, already?
I don't forget to swim: I want to hold the scent of sea
    all the way back in my half sleep.

I buy a possum jumper, sheepskin boots, Tim Tams,
    a wildflower tea-towel; there's sea sponge in my hair.
The last day people on the street look like those I once knew:
    women in coffee shops remind me of my long ago mother.

I bump into a lover's best friend who's from so far in the past
    that we just watch the small surprise.
The last day I take photos of street signs, verandahs, roadsides,
    a dog who seems to know me well,

a house I lived in twenty years ago overgrown with bushes
    as if they waited for me to come
before they can be cut down. There's an ache
    behind my eyes and I can't remember all the heaviness

I first drove through the city with, saying a little too loudly
    to myself, to the bus driver, anyone,
that I do not live here any more and my god returning
    has been a long time coming.

Samovar

In the winter, doves fly over Petersburg
and I look at the pigeons on the ground,
stepping over ice, stepping into snow,
pacing, waiting, for no one in particular.

The babushkas hand me cinnamon tea,
saying, 'You'll be warmer soon.
You'll be warmer.'
I wait as glass after glass
rests between my palms.

But still I shiver, staring
impatiently, staring at my book –
no – at the cathedral across the road,
its onion domes – no –
at the cracking paint and broken
tiles along the wall.

Tea and tea and tea, and then he sits.
There. Finally. Thank God,
but there is no God in Saint Petersburg.
Instead, there's Lenin and Pavlova
and the man sitting across from me, Mitya,
man with the beard.

At the apartment we have more tea.
Through the window a golden spire shines,
a cathedral by a prison
where Dostoevsky once lingered in isolation's dark,
but I could leave, if I wanted to.
If outside the pigeons weren't calling my name.

If inside, Mitya wasn't, either.

Cold again, I shake in his arms,
tremble as he embraces me.
'You're a keeper,' he says. 'You're a keeper.'

Interview Conducted through the Man-Eater's Throat

Are you in there, friend?
Like the blue-black char in a chimney.
If I crane my neck at the windpipe's flue,
I can see a far sky framed
in teeth, a double horseshoe
of mauve lips, and there's your face
bent toward my trouble. I'm the fresh inch
of ash in the furnace,
a twist of smoke where the stack is bent.

What happened to you, friend?
My whole life happened. I was napping
by an open window, sun
on my back through mosquito netting
while a hired boy strummed
the guitar. For a long time nothing
happened. Then a chord went wrong.
I felt a shadow and turned to a knifing
smile that devoured my yawn.

Friend, friend, were you taking precautions?
I slaughtered clean goats on an altar
of antlers, gave Caesar's
to Caesar, remembered my Psalter.
I installed a procedure
for the watchmen's patrols: their whistles
were nickel, they carried red beacons.
Each guard wore a sword and a pistol.
I swore I was safe, and still I was eaten.

Friend, what happened?
The great mouth happened
and the rough red tongue.
Now this little room happens
where a lantern's hung
above a small square table and a wicker
stool squats by the throbbing wall.
Someone's lived here before: a flask
and matches in a wooden bowl.

The beast is sleeping. Can you climb out, friend?
Past those teeth in their ivory
rows, the gash of gums,
those livid tonsils? Even if I dared, every
time he coughs my grip comes
free in offal. And before you ask, that fiery
sinkhole in the corner is worse. It flexes
and sparks: an acid catalogue, a diary
in gastric stinks. These are not exits.

Well, what are your plans, friend?
I believe I'm meant to wait at the table.
I'll sample the whisky and host
this little lottery that's straddled
on the monster's gut. The roasted
stool wants company. I'll play a solitaire
that contemplates the well-gnawed
rubble for a sign: how a prayer
busies itself inside the cluttered ears of God.

Friend, what is that noise?
Outside, you can hear that rumbling?
He's waking up and he's hungry.
That noise wants empires tumbling
down a throat. It's the jangling
of relics in a pocket of lung and I'm coming
to understand it. I'm not angry
now or even scared. I think something's
being chewed on that will change me.

Forgetting How to Swim

O element that was my element,
where did it come from? This hostility –
as if I only didn't drown by accident,

somehow above what nourished me
in utero. Amphibious impostor,
my visa marked 'Returning to the Sea'

did not convince its briny officers
the day of my rejection from the Regnitz,
all panicked breath and blubbered paternosters.

Lurching ashore in boxers, one foot nicked
and trailing blood like Grendel,
inarticulate in hubris

(Sir Politic returning to his shell)
without a phone, my glasses or the language,
I knew I had good reasons to be grateful.

Being on dry land is a privilege,
as is so rarely needing to tread water
or struggle just to stay above the surface.

I look at my own life like a reporter,
surprised to see how many small enchantments
invisibly have lifted me from danger.

IN A LOCAL CAFÉ

If sometimes Odysseus used to talk about Ithaca,
now he has stopped.
Two or three peels of mandarin
and one stick of cinnamon
in a nearly-empty mug of a local café
is everything that reminds him of home this Christmas.

Many compasses and horizons have gone by,
maybe right ones, maybe wrong ones.
Maybe their needle has been magnetized dangerously
by exotic marabous and local cafés.
How easily a needle can be dazzled
on never-ending horizons.

In the background carols and melodies are heard
in a language that sounds nothing like childhood.
Years when the dreams knew very well
how to perch on songs and hummingbirds.

Now the needle points permanently at home.
It has learnt to baptize every image as a memory:
the nicely faded mistletoe we never had,
the Christmas coffee you never drank.
And the memories are beginning to look like dense veils
making Ithaca's banks nearly invisible in the fog.

Skype

That it's strange to miss home
and be in it – its mnemonic

of rooms.
There you are

landlocked,
a wink away through fibre optics packed

underground like rhizomes.
In a satellite view of Europe I dream of

from the east,
the slide rule of shadow

draws across from the western
wall of the Kremlin.

Light here swells
against the kitchen

window. We trade a word
of your language for a word

of mine when my mother's voice
interjects – *boast*

it says, in a sense I've heard
only her ever use to mean

convex; swollen,
as of something holding something else in.

How strange she speaks
as air transferred lissom through the patio.

How strange home
does not stay as it's left.

Her voice is a mist
of dust on the sill.

In Russian, I learn
to want.

I want.
I want

a tinkle of cutlery,
flowers in that vase.

Rather I plant this word
in your language.

I bury her again
as a bulb in your throat

somewhere in the suburbs
of Moscow.

ENGLAND, WHERE DID YOU GO?

England of the burrow-in green, chalk galvanized giant,
undulating earth-bank fortress, flinted Roman wall,
full flair gorse, messy hay-trails waiting
to be bin-bag-baled by steel mandibles:

you unroll through the window of a train,
but should I get out in search of you, you'd be off,
and I'd be left wandering down dual carriageways,
looking across bean fields and filthy ditches.

The Descent from Mount Olympus

Where to begin? Maybe after the centuries
in earth, your power leaking into dark, when
a rough-palmed farmer knocked his plough
against your neck, hauled you to heat
and scent of dittany. Bargained over, saved
from the Turks, crated, cranked aboard without
due care so that you broke in half and lost
two limbs which ghost-ache in the northern chill.

Or start perhaps with the man from Antioch
unlocking you from rock, chip by considered
chip, until you stood, torso twisted, right hand
offering a pomegranate, draped sacrum to foot
in rigid folds with belly, breasts and shoulders
bare to Anatolian air.

No. Let's begin in the time of cherishing, high
on a hill, in a citadel where white doves picked
at votive corn, then crooned in sweet-oiled myrtles;
where you received the prayers of those
who sought to find or keep true love, and
offerings of women longing for a child. Was it
Hephaistos' rage or Athens' battering rams
that crushed your shrine to brash?

So, all the beginnings are told. Now there's
no chime of orioles or crush of thyme beneath
the feet of acolytes and only a cleaner's cloth
to tease from throat to waist, draw spirals round
your navel. Never the touch of loving hands.
This is how it ends.

BEFORE

No one leaves home unless home is the mouth of a shark.
           – Warsan Shire

Before

Before *illegal*
Before becoming the influx, the scar, the stain
Before finding my new name in a scuffed English novel
Before *Jane*
Before mastering the sturdy handshake
Before never using it
Before swallowing the lilts of my own tongue
Before forcing my mouth to *e-nun-ci-ate*
Before being misunderstood
Before dreaming of my mother's songs
Before learning the spirals of British decorum
Before *cup of tea, anyone?*
Before yearning for a belonging I could name

Before the sound of my laugh began to decay
Before the grope of cheap polyester
Before my prayers mocked me
Before *go home* ricocheted from mouths to vans
Before dreams of going home
Before each footstep became an apology
Before *how destitute exactly?*
Before *not destitute enough*
Before *application refused*
Before disinfecting floors
Before cash in hand
Before temporary

Before knowing
Before the stain
Before the scar
Before the influx
Before illegal

Before

Common Prayer

Crocodile skin or a large snake,
polished by hands, carried in pockets;
it has a buttoned pocket for the collection coin,
on the flyleaf my mother's maiden name
in blue fountain pen, 1932.

I've kept it since she died.
She kept it after gran died,
who held on to it after granddad died
in the garage in '51.
They'd kept it since she left home
(the war delayed everything)
and went up to college, married, miscarried.
She'd had it, we know, since she was nine,
the year she left Lisbon on a white ocean liner
with her mother and breaking father
sailing to England and slow decline.

Inside the pocket, my heart leaps, a coin,
sixpence of 1951 – but the detail, the king's hair
worn, condition not even Fine. She put it there
years later, I guess. Pre-decimalisation.

Search for more clues. The bookmark ribbon
opens on Communion – was she confirmed?
Rifle through the Rizla-thin pages for notes
or underlinings, a turned-down corner.
Nothing but hymn after hymn after hymn.

Back Home

You did not want to come back here
but it is home.
Familiar exile to which you return
every time you and yet another
do not work out.
Here because it was the first and last place
it was okay to scream it isn't fair
stamp upstairs
slam doors and cry.
It is cheap.

Save the rent you pay in making tea
and staying up late listening to your mother
cuss out your father
who's fallen asleep in his dinner again.
You sit
crony woman-daughter
sipping from chipped china
nodding out a painful £600 a month including bills
and how much she wants a divorce
but can't afford one
so they still sleep in the same bed.

VENA CAVA

when it rains here
I can pretend it's home

outside, the sky is a cloud
and my hand is condensed with water

from touching walls
of earth

roots weave into my hair
I might stay here

learn to love
the rank air

taking my lungs
wipe the slate

clean of rescue

TEN YEARS LATER
IN A DIFFERENT BAR

The city has changed like cities do;
the bar where we sang has closed.
We have changed like cities do.

There is an alley where the young, the new
drink their beer in sun-drenched clothes.
The city has changed like cities do.

We once drank beers on the street too –
the bars too small for the dreams we chose.
We have changed like cities do.

Graffiti on the walls, red blazing blue,
says this city is more poetry than prose.
The city has changed like cities do.

Laure and I light up, smoke a few,
search for what we dropped here: shadows.
We have changed like cities do.

The liquid light reminds me of you,
the laughter, the ceiling pipes – who knows
if the city has changed like cities do,
if we have changed like cities do.

Marooned

All your things have been taken
away. Here is your island of salt,

what's left – your aged body, your pocked
mind, a horizon that glimmers blank.

Still you imagine, and try
where you're tossed – to build again:

shelter, table, food, garment,
stumble, think it through. You know time

is brief. Some boat will come
with dark oars and ghost captain.

Like a fool, you stand ankle deep
in the sea, waving it in.

ACKNOWLEDGEMENTS

'Light on the Galactic Tide', by Anja Konig, was first published in *Heavenly Bodies* (Beautiful Dragons, 2014).

'Dundalk', by Frank Dullaghan, was previously published in his collection *Enough Light to See the Dark* (Cinnamon Press, 2012) and *The SHOp* (Winter 2010).

'Emigrant', by Carole Bromley, was previously published in *Smiths Knoll* and her collection *A Guided Tour of the Ice House* (Smith/Doorstop, 2011).

'Prodigalia', by George David Clark, was previously published in *Pleiades* 33.1 in 2013.

'Coming down', by Elizabeth Horne, was first published in the anthology *And the whole damned thing* (Poetzinc, 2003).

'Away', by Carole Bromley, won second prize in the New Forest Poetry Competition and was first published in the New Forest Poets anthology.

'Coming Home', by Ellie Danak, was published in an earlier form in *Poetry Nook*, Vol. 1 (Plum White Press LLC, 2013).

'Ariel', by Charlotte Higgins, was first published in the anthology *Lines Underwater* (Poems Underwater/Tyburn Tree, 2013).

'Winged Carrots', by Zeina Hashem Beck, was first published in her collection *To Live in Autumn* (The Backwaters Press, 2014). It has also been published in *Not Somewhere*

Else But Here: A Contemporary Anthology of Women & Place (Sundress Publication, 2014).

'The Terminal Building', by Carole Bromley, was first published in *Smiths Knoll*.

'Interview Conducted through the Man-Eater's Throat', by George David Clark, was previously published in *Pleiades* 33.1 in 2013.

'England, where did you go?', by Holly Hopkins, was first published in *The Times Literary Supplement* in 2014.

'The Descent from Mount Olympus', by Gill Learner, was first published in *The Agister's Experiment* (Two Rivers Press, 2011).

'Before', by Selina Nwulu, was first published online, as part of the New Left Project poetry collection in 2013.

'vena cava', by Ivy Alvarez, previously appeared in her first collection, *Mortal* (Red Morning Press, 2006).

'Ten years later in a different bar', by Zeina Hashem Beck, was previously published in her collection *To Live in Autumn* (The Backwaters Press, 2014).

ABOUT THE POETS

Ivy Alvarez is the author of two poetry collections: *Disturbance* (Seren Books, 2013) and *Mortal* (Red Morning Press, 2006). A recipient of writing residencies from MacDowell Colony, Hawthornden Castle and Fundación Valparaiso, her work has been published in many countries, with poems translated into Russian, Spanish, Japanese and Korean.

Zeina Hashem Beck is a Lebanese poet. Her first book, *To Live in Autumn* (The Backwaters Press, 2014), won the 2013 Backwaters Prize, judged by Lola Haskins. Her poems have appeared or are forthcoming in *Ploughshares*, *Nimrod*, *Poetry Northwest* and *Mslexia*, among others. She lives in Dubai with her husband and two daughters.

Alex Bell grew up in Northumberland and Dorset. She now lives and works in London, where she never feels homesick for the countryside. Her work has appeared in *Magma*, *The Rialto* and *Poetry Wales*.

Carole Bromley is a Creative Writing tutor at York University. Her poems have been widely published and her first collection, *A Guided Tour of the Ice House,* was published by Smith/Doorstop in 2011. Carole has won a number of first prizes, including The Bridport, Yorkshire Open and Bronte Society Literary Prize. She was shortlisted in the 2014 Manchester Writing for Children Prize.

Mary Buchinger is the author of *Aerialist* (forthcoming with Gold Wake Press in 2015; shortlisted for the May Swenson Poetry Award, OSU Press/The Journal Wheeler Prize for Poetry and Perugia Press Prize). She received the

Varoujan and Houghton Awards from the New England Poetry Club and is Associate Professor of English/Communication Studies, MCPHS University, Boston, Massachusetts.

George David Clark teaches creative writing at Valparaiso University and his first book, *Reveille*, won the 2014 Miller Williams Prize. His most recent poems can be found in *Alaska Quarterly Review, Antioch Review, The Believer, Blackbird, FIELD, Yale Review* and elsewhere. The editor of *32 Poems*, he lives in Indiana.

James Coghill has had poems published in places such as *Popshot Magazine, Ink, Sweat & Tears, The Cadaverine, Lighthouse, Verse Kraken* and *Orbis*. He is currently working on a pamphlet of animal/ecopoems; as such, writing about something more people-shaped is a welcome holiday.

Ellie Danak is a poet with a background in researching modern Swedish crime novels and skiing off hills head first. She lives and writes in Edinburgh and divides her time between her notebooks and her toddler son. She blogs at Poetry & Pandemonium.

An Australian who lives in London, **Cath Drake** has been published in the UK, Australia and US. In 2012, she was short-listed for the Venture Poetry Award and was writer in residence at the Albany Arts Centre café. Cath's pamphlet *Sleeping with Rivers* won the 2013 Mslexia/Seren poetry pamphlet prize and was the Poetry Book Society Summer Choice in 2014.

Frank Dullaghan holds an MA with Distinction in Writing (University of South Wales). He co-founded the *Essex Poetry Festival*, edited *Seam Poetry Magazine,* and his third poetry collection, *The Same Roads Back*, is due out with Cinnamon Press in September 2014. He lives in Dubai and also writes short screen and stage plays.

John Froy lives in Reading where he works as a painter decorator. He has published a collection of poems, *Eggshell* (Two Rivers Press, 2007), and two volumes of memoir: *70 Waterloo Road* and *The Art School Dance* (Two Rivers Press, 2010 and 2013 respectively).

Charlotte Higgins was born in Belfast and now lives in Cambridge. A previous winner of the Foyle Young Poets of the Year Award (2010, commended) and SLAMbassadors (2011), she has performed in the Royal Festival Hall, at the Proms, and at Nuyorican Poetry Café. She runs Speakeasy, a Cambridge poetry night.

Holly Hopkins lives in London where she is reading an MA in Creative Writing at Royal Holloway. Holly won an Eric Gregory Award in 2011 and her debut pamphlet, *Soon Every House Will Have One*, won the 2014 Poetry Business Pamphlet Competition and was Poetry Book Society Pamphlet Choice.

In 2013, Australian poet **Elizabeth Horne** won the Tom Collins Poetry Prize and was shortlisted for the Australian Science Poetry Prize. She has been published in Australian journals including *Meanjin, Famous Reporter, Blue Dog Australian Poetry* and the *New England Review*. She is also a printmaker and children's writer.

Anja Konig grew up in the German language and now writes in English. Her poetry has appeared in the UK and the US in magazines and anthologies such as *Poetry Review,*

Poetry London, Magma, The Manhattan Review and *Cimarron Review*. Her first pamphlet, *Advice for an Only Child,* will be published by Flipped Eye Publishing in 2014.

Eve Lacey is the editor of *Furies*, an anthology of contemporary women's poetry published in 2014. She was awarded the David Almond Fellowship in 2012 and longlisted for the Hot Key Young Writers Prize in 2013. Her poetry was published in *The Emma Press Anthology of Motherhood* in 2014.

Gill Learner's poetry has been widely published since 2002, most recently in *Acumen, Mslexia* and *Poetry News* Spring 2014. Gill has also won several awards, including the Hamish Canham Prize 2008 and the Buxton Poetry Competition 2011 & 2012. Her first collection is *The Agister's Experiment* (Two Rivers Press, 2011).

Rachel Long is a writer, poet and spoken word artist based in London. She has read at the Olympic stadium and Royal Festival Hall, and has been commissioned by Apples & Snakes, SPOKE and Clayground Collective. Rachel is a proud member of international poetry collective Burn After Reading and she is currently studying an MA in Creative and Life Writing at Goldsmith's University London.

Marissa Mazek is a Creative Writing MFA candidate at Hollins University in Virginia. Her work has appeared in *Watershed Review, The Rampallian* and other publications. She received an Honorable Mention in Glimmer Train's December 2013 Fiction Open, and is an alumna of Barnard College, Columbia University.

John McCullough's first collection *The Frost Fairs* (Salt, 2011) won the Polari First Book Prize for 2012. It was a

Book of the Year for both the *Independent* and The Poetry School, and a summer read for the *Observer*. He lives in Hove, and teaches creative writing for the Open University.

Cheryl Moskowitz is a US-born, UK-based, prize-winning poet, translator and novelist. Her poems have been published in literary journals including *Poetry Review, Magma* and *Artemis*. Her books include a novel, *Wyoming Trail*, poems for children, *Can it Be About Me*, and her poetry collection *The Girl is Smiling*.

Selina Nwulu is a writer and poet, often inspired by global justice, protest and politics. Selina has toured nationally with Apples and Snakes and she has been published in magazines and anthologies, including *In Protest: 150 Poems for Human Rights* (Institute of Commonwealth Studies, 2013). Her first collection is due to be published by Burning Eye in 2015.

Richard O'Brien's home is in Lincolnshire, though he has also lived in Oxford, Nantes, France and, currently, Stratford-upon-Avon. His work has appeared in *Poetry London, The Best British Poetry 2013*, and three pamphlets, including *The Emmores* (The Emma Press) and *A Bloody Mess* (Dead Ink/Valley Press), both published in 2014.

Lisa Ortiz's poems have appeared in *Best New Poets 2013, Zyzzyva, The Literary Review*, and have been featured on *Verse Daily*. She wrote 'Marooned' while living in Peru, but by the time you read this she has likely returned to her home town of Santa Cruz, California.

Rachel Piercey is an editor at *The Cadaverine* magazine and The Emma Press. Her illustrated pamphlet of love poems, *The Flower and the Plough*, was published by The

Emma Press in 2013 and a second pamphlet, *Rivers Wanted*, is forthcoming in October 2014.

Stephen Sexton lives in Belfast, where he studies at the Seamus Heaney Centre for Poetry. His poems have appeared in *Poetry London, The Honest Ulsterman, Poetry Ireland Review, The Ulster Tatler*, and as part of the Lifeboat Series of readings based in Belfast. He was the winner of the inaugural FSNI National Poetry Competition and his first pamphlet, *Oils*, is publishing with The Emma Press in October 2014.

Vili Skarlopoulou is from Athens, Greece but currently lives in London. She studied classical literature in both Athens and London. Her poems have appeared in various magazines including *Myths of The Near Future, The Cadaverine* magazine and *Young Poets Network*.

James Trevelyan grew up in the Midlands and now lives in South London. Having completed an MA in Creative Writing at Royal Holloway, his poems have been published in *14 Magazine, Cake, The Cadaverine* magazine, and anthologised in *Bedford Square* 5. He is currently an Administrator at the Poetry Book Society.

The Emma Press

small press, big dreams

The Emma Press is an independent publisher dedicated to producing books which are sweet, funny and beautiful. It was founded in 2012 in Winnersh, UK, by Emma Wright and the first Emma Press book, *The Flower and the Plough* by Rachel Piercey, was published in January 2013.

Our current publishing programme includes a mixture of themed poetry anthologies and single-author pamphlets, with an ongoing engagement with the works of the Roman poet Ovid. We publish poems and books which excite us, and we are often on the lookout for new writing to feature in our latest projects.

Visit our website and sign up to the Emma Press newsletter to hear about all upcoming calls for submissions as well as our events and publications. You can also purchase our other titles and poetry-related stationery in our online shop.

http://theemmapress.com

The Emma Press Anthology of Motherhood

ISBN: 978 0 9574596 7 0

Price: £10 / $17

Love and devotion sit alongside exhaustion and doubt in this profoundly moving collection of poems about mothers and the state of motherhood.

Edited by Rachel Piercey and Emma Wright, with poems from Deborah Alma, Stephanie Arsoska, Liz Berry, Sara Boyes, Carole Bromley, Laura Chalar, George David Clark, Flora de Falbe, Kate Garrett, Hilary Gilmore, Melinda Kallasmae, David Kennedy, Anna Kirk, Anna Kisby, Peter LaBerge, Eve Lacey, Anna Leader, Marena Lear, Katherine Lockton, Rachel Long, Julie Maclean, Ikhda Ayuning Maharsi, Kathryn Maris, Richard O'Brien, Rachel Piercey, Clare Pollard, Jacqueline Saphra, Kathryn Simmonds, Lavinia Singer, Catherine Smith, Camellia Stafford and Megan Watkins.

THE EMMA PRESS ANTHOLOGY OF FATHERHOOD

ISBN: 978 1 910139 00 4

Price: £10 / $17

A deeply affecting collection of poems about fathers and fatherhood, exploring themes of joy, masculinity, expectations, disappointment and deep love.

Edited by Rachel Piercey and Emma Wright, with poems from Alan Buckley, John Canfield, Oliver Comins, Nathan Curnow, Hugh Dunkerley, Flora de Falbe, Sarah Fletcher, John Fuller, Jeremy Grant, John Grey, Robert Hamberger, James Harris, Sara Hirsch, Lynn Hoffman, Kirsten Irving, Max Maher, Martin Malone, Harry Man, Katrina Naomi, Richard O'Brien, Rachel Piercey, Stevie Ronnie, Jacqueline Saphra, John Saunders, Tom Sheehan, Di Slaney, Jon Stone, Richard Thompson and Jerrold Yam.

A Poetic Primer for Love and Seduction: Naso was my Tutor

ISBN: 978 0 9574596 3 2
Price: £10 / $17
The Emma Press Ovid

Romantic adventurers! Look no further for your new handbook, your trusty adviser in matters of the heart, bedroom and boudoir. Forget the Game! Ditch the Rules! The Poetic Primer contains all you need to know about love, seduction, relationships and heartbreak. Inspired by Roman poet Ovid's *Ars Amatoria* (The Art of Lovemaking) and *Remedia Amoris* (The Cure for Love).

Edited by Rachel Piercey and Emma Wright, with poems from Jo Brandon, John Canfield, Jade Cuttle, Amy Key, Anja Konig, Cheryl Moskowitz, Abigail Parry, Rachel Piercey, Richard O'Brien, Christopher Reid, Jacqueline Saphra, Liane Strauss, Nicola Warwick, Ruth Wiggins and Andrew Wynn Owen.

THE EMMA PRESS ANTHOLOGY OF MILDLY EROTIC VERSE

ISBN: 978 0 9574596 2 5
Price: £10 / $17

A beautiful anthology which celebrates modern eroticism in all its messy, sexy glory. We see lovers imagined as heroes and hares; describing what they want in jawdropping detail (or maybe with no words at all); meeting at swimming pools, sinking into baths and magic boxes. They wonder about lost knickers, worry about caravans, and – sometimes – find themselves transformed.

Edited by Rachel Piercey and Emma Wright, with poems from Julia Bird, Mel Denham, Joy Donnell, Hugh Dunkerley, Kirsten Irving, Amy Key, Anja Konig, Ikhda Ayuning Maharsi, Julie Mullen, Richard O'Brien, Emma Reay, Kristen Roberts, Jacqueline Saphra, Lawrence Schimel, Stephen Sexton, Jon Stone, Sara-Mae Tuson, Ruth Wiggins and Jerrold Yam.

The Dead Snail Diaries
by Jamie McGarry

ISBN: 978 0 9574596 9 4
Price: £8.50 / $15

A beguiling collection of observational poems and literary parodies about snail culture, as told by a prematurely-crushed snail poet and translated by Jamie McGarry.

Captain Love and the Five Joaquins
by John Clegg

ISBN: 978 1 910139 01 1
Price: £5 / $9

A thrilling adventure story which follows the progress of bounty hunter Harry Love on his tour of California with the supposed head of horse-thief Joaquin Murrieta in a jar.

ALSO FROM THE EMMA PRESS

THE HELD AND THE LOST, *by Kristen Roberts*

ISBN: 978 0 9574596 8 7 – PRICE: £5 / $9

A moving collection of distinctly Australian poems about love,
marriage and family life.

RASPBERRIES FOR THE FERRY, *by Andrew Wynn Owen*

ISBN: 978 0 9574596 5 6 – PRICE: £6.50 / $12

Andrew Wynn Owen dazzles in his debut pamphlet, whisking
the reader up with his infectious rhythms and lively sensuality.

IKHDA, BY IKHDA, *by Ikhda Ayuning Maharsi*

ISBN: 978 0 9574596 6 3 – PRICE: £6.50 / $12

Reading this book is like being splashed with freezing water and
showered with popping candy and wild roses.

OILS, *by Stephen Sexton*

Publishing October 2014

Belfast poet Stephen Sexton evokes melancholy and a strange
kind of romance throughout his brilliant debut pamphlet.

RIVERS WANTED, *by Rachel Piercey*

Publishing October 2014

Rachel Piercey charms and disturbs in this beautiful, frequently
heart-breaking collection of poems about love, identity and home.